UNTIED SATIRES

A NOTE TO ONE SELF

SNEHA TYAGI

Copyright © Sneha Tyagi
All Rights Reserved.

Everybody who has something to say but is unable to convey it deserves dedication. It is intended for you, who are constrained by words and thoughts. Those tied satires could be untied at any time, so perhaps you are reading this now in the hopes that it will help you untie your own knotted satires.

Contents

Preface

Every reader may understand this book's clear writing. The reader's perception affects how the meanings are interpreted. These little poems were inspired by satires on daily life that I believe I may unravel through this book.

1. Her Untiring Tries

I was too hard on myself
I was too hard on myself putting on questions
Putting on and on questions
The questions that even didn't deseverved to be answered
The questions were becoming hard on myself
The question was for the love
The love about which I was questioning the world
The love if it existed or not
The love if existed was for me or not
When I got the answer I was too hard on myself
It was me who was questioning the answer
I was too hard on myself.

2. A Letter to you

Why do I love you?
I was that abandoned puppy
with shiny eyes of hope
you gave me shelter
in the warmth of your love
Not its hard to leave you.

3. She

She who wanted to fly high
She wanted to touch the sky
She worked hard tirelessly for her dreams
She unknowingly got into a process
She now whose wings were turned red
She who needs our support
She whose wings were made heavy by society
She has the hope to once again fly the same.

4. The Choice

That day I thought this day will be the best
To this day I miss that day when I used to be grateful every day
On this day I want many things don't know for which day
That day I had everything
This day I want many things which I don't want but I want to
show that I have those things
Is it a limitation or a mirror to myself that doesn't even show
me?

5. The Confusion

The best person or the better me
He is the epitome of love, sincerity, trust, loyalty, care, and
whatnot.
He is the better me...
He taught me, love, he taught me about the world
He became my world in a very short time
Is he the best person or the better me?
He is the peace that I search for the whole of my day.
He is the beauty that everyone would compel to admire.
He is the better me
Do you know who he is?
The person reading these lines you
My love.

6. Imagination

Imagination is the better version of reality
Imagination the positivity
Imagination the hope
Imagination the expectation
Imagination the acceptance
Imagination my happy place
Imagination the uniting activity
Imagination is a never-ending game
Imagination on my always winning ng place
Imagination the ray of hope
Imagination the peace music
Imagination far from reality
Imagination is my reality
Or this reality is my imagination?
Please clear this my love as you are the oin ne my imagination
and reality.

7. The Journey

On the way to you
My beauty lies on the way to you
Sometimes when I get lost
I find my direction on the way to you
My way is on the way to you
By many leaps and bounds
I Jump and grump
I find my happiness on the way to you
My destination is on the way to you.

8. Flyers

It was with me I thought
It will stay the same I thought
It will stay for long I thought
It will never leave me I thought
It will stay the same I thought.

9. Tying and Untying

The feelings are tied

The words are tyed

The expressions are tied

The emotions are tied

The world outside you is untyed

The World within you is tied

And

Here are your tries to bridge the distance between the tied and

tyed.

10. Separation

From me to you
the distance now awaits to be covered
From me to you.
Those long satires upon which we walked days and nights
are apart From me to you.
The Flyer wants to get back to when we were together
and promised to sail through every satire of future
From me to you.

Untyed Satires

Each of us has satires that will endure for a very long time. The satire that endures throughout our own lives. They must be moved from being tied to being untied. Let all of those feelings and emotions out, and then everyone should write their own Untyed Satire.